rhapsody 2022

an anthology of guelph writing

Vocamus Press
Guelph, Ontario

Presented by Vocamus Writers Community

Published by Vocamus Press

Edited by Michael Kleiza

Cover image by David J. Knight

ISBN 13: 978-1-77422-090-0 (pbk)
ISBN 13: 978-1-77422-091-7 (ebk)

VP

Vocamus Press
130 Dublin Street, North
Guelph, Ontario, Canada
N1H 4N4

www.vocamus.net

2022

Preface

The Rhapsody Anthology is an annual collection of Guelph and area poetry presented by Vocamus Writers Community, a non-profit community organization that supports literary culture in Guelph, Ontario.

The anthology is a celebration of local writing that includes both authors who are well established in their craft and those who are published here for the first time, reflecting the writers and writing that formed the literary communities of Guelph during the years 2020/2021 and 2021/2022.

This is a special edition of the anthology for at least three reasons. First, because it collects the poems that were submitted over a two year span, catching up for the year that covid prevented publication, and so it contains more than one poem by certain authors. Second, because for the first time in many years it once again contains very short fiction as well as poetry. And third, because it's the anthology's final edition, the purposes of *Rhapsody* having been in many ways superseded by other programs.

The collection was edited by Michael Kleiza. The cover art was provided by David J. Knight. The cover and interior were designed by Jeremy Luke Hill.

Acknowledgments

The Rhapsody Anthology is produced by Vocamus Writers Community, a non-profit community organization that supports writing, publishing, and book culture in the Guelph area.

Over the period of this anthology, our work has been generously supported by Arboretum Press, June Blair, Candace de Taeye, Carol Dilworth, Sheri Doyle, The Elora Poetry Centre, Nikki Everts-Hammond, Alec Follett, Martina Freitag, J. A. Gibbens, Mary Jo Gordon, Joanne Guidoccio, Larry Harder, Clifford Jackman, Kathleen James, Carole Kennedy, Laura Lush, Donna McCaw, Melissa McGrath, Marianne Micros, Debra NIcholson, Allison Playfair, Greg Rhyno, J. R. Tim Struthers, and several other anonymous donors. We appreciate their contributions to the production of this volume and the work of our organization. If you'd also like to support the work of Vocamus Writers Community you can do so by searching us on www.fundrazr.com.

Thanks to Michael Kleiza for editing the collection. Thanks to all the contributors for sharing their work so generously. Thanks to Tudor Costache for allowing his photograph to be used for the book cover. Thanks finally to all those who contribute to the literary culture of Guelph as readers, writers, publishers, sponsors, venues, broadcasters, and in countless other ways – this collection is a celebration of all that you do.

rhapsody 2022

an anthology of guelph writing

Table of Contents

Penis 1
Darcy Hiltz

Poem Now 2
Valerie Senyk

An Old Judge Imagines the Afterlife 3
James Clarke

Eramosa River 4
Nicholas Ruddock

Two Haiku 5
Rashmeet Kaur

At the Beach 6
Bieke Stengos

So Happy To Be 7
Kathryn Edgecomb

Kelpie 8
Tom Vaine

The Symphonic River 9
Jerry Prager

every town needs a poet 11
Morvern McNie

Hope 13
Melinda Burns

Dining in Restaurant   15
Sheri Doyle

Oncolomancy   16
Jeremy Luke Hill

May 4, 2020 Poem   17
Sandy Bassie

**To the Resident of the House at the Top
of Dublin St.**   19
Kate MacDonald

Getting Through   20
Donna McCaw

Back Then   21
Michael Kleiza

Silent Killer   22
Darcy Hiltz

Memorial for a Nameless Matriarch   23
Shayne Coffin

Mouth   24
Valerie Senyk

Lost Poetry   25
Trish Heyes

How to Survive Winter (Tip #12)   26
Serena Tene

For Pam   28
Catherine Reilly

Am I   **29**
    Darcy Hiltz

Immanence   **30**
    Marian Thorpe

Saturday Special   **31**
    Anne Walk

Penis

Darcy Hiltz

Darcy Hiltz is an Archivist / Librarian at Guelph Public Library. He writes, through his FaceBook profile, about genealogy and information management, and in his spare time he writes poetry. He is married and lives in Fergus, Ontario.

Penis

shrivels
    glans
    head, tip
      vanishes

as if foreskin exists

i

 d
   i
     g

coach it out
like a cat
that hides
under the bed
p u l l
soft tissue back
until the head
          peaks

s
  t
   r
    e
     a
       m
        s

            pee

1

Poem Now

Valerie Senyk

Valerie Senyk is a writer, multi-media artist, a playwright, an actor, and a performance poet. She has published a full-length volume of poetry, I Want A Poem *(Vocamus Press, 2014).*

Poem Now

There was uncertainty
then my shirt changed and the rust
coloured-spots reversed
and flapped in the wind

There was uncertainty
then I folded my arms cross-wise
like a salted pretzel
wondering when?

There was uncertainty
though the garden grew as
per usual greening
feeding others gladly

There was uncertainty
but if I knew it I
didn't know it as I
tried to walk backwards

feeling quite blind

An Old Judge Imagines the Afterlife

James Clarke

James Clarke was born in Peterborough, Ontario and attended McGill University and Osgoode Hall. He practiced law in Cobourg, Ontario and served as a judge of the Superior Court of Ontario. He is now retired, residing in Guelph, Ontario. He is the author of many volumes of poetry and several memoirs.

An Old Judge Imagines the Afterlife

It comes down to this – there is no official
schedule for fulfillment in the afterlife nor

ideals to sour. The cascade of courtroom
argument no longer drums on the nerves or

dampens the spirit. In the spirit-flesh of
pure being to see is to take, to wish for

to have, everything calm, measured, exact.
Here all have answered the one important

question: what have you done with your
one & only life, paid the deep price of

admission. Old judges just float from day
to day peering through the rusty keyhole

of law, praying for those left behind, every
night a promise of rest for those, blessed &

blessing, who have learned how to live.

Eramosa River

Nicholas Ruddock

Nicholas Ruddock is author of The Parabolist *(Doubleday 2010),* How Loveta Got Her Baby *(Breakwater 2014),* ight Ambulance *(Breakwater 2016), and* The Last Hummingbird West of Chile *(Breakwater 2021).*

Eramosa River

Once I lived by the side of the Eramosa River
with my mother and father and the woods surround,
we'd swim in the current and fish in the shallows,
and watch raccoons hunt the crayfish down.
Cool was the water where I learned to swim,
spring by the millpond, dragonfly skim,
red-tailed the hawk plummeting down,
circle of feathers askance on the ground,
thunder and lightning, hail and snow,
calendar turning—ten years ago—
a cottage, three windows, a candle, a well,
stove run on wood, quarter-moon spell,
the heron, the waxwing, the paddle, the sigh,
mist from the cedars, kingfisher cry,
marigold, crocus, sumac blood-red,
bulrushes, catkins, asleep in our beds,
ice jam, ice cracking, the owl and the mouse
wind in the larches, branch scraping the house,
dark eyes at the window pane, river gone wild,
sweepers with fingers, awakening child
until we moved to the city, to Liverpool Street,
and all of a sudden it was people we'd meet,
a postman, a neighbour, the sidewalk back home,
fox and the marten, left on their own,
the moon rising slowly from the Campbellville
Road,
bats swooping lowly as stars explode,
my parents and I, three years we would spend
on the Eramosa River, shimmer and bend.

Two Haiku

Rashmeet Kaur

Rashmeet Kaur is an undergraduate student at the University of Guelph completing a Bachelor of Science degree with a Bio-Medical Science major. She merges her passion for both the sciences and the humanities through her poetry and mixed media artwork, which has been published in Kaleidoscope *and* Margins Magazine.

Two Haiku

My yellow tiptoes
Aligned with: You are loved, scrawled
In white sidewalk chalk

And for a moment
I stood still, in the warmth of
Almost believing

At the Beach

Bieke Stengos

Bieke was born in Belgium, came to Canada as a young woman, and has lived here ever since, with time spent in various countries overseas. She has published a chapbook, Aunt Ida, *two collections of poetry,* Abandoned by the Muse *and* Transmigrator.

At the Beach

Gentle footfall on soft sand,
rat-tat-tat of goose wings.
Noise preceding, vision later,
but, for now nothing, but
gentle lapping of water on sand.

Barrages like staccato,
lament of distant loon.
Vision now, mourning later
but, for now nothing, but
gentle breakers on bodies

softening in glassy waves.
Horizon dissolving
lone bird, for now,
on an expanse of water,
breathing out.

So Happy To Be

Kathryn Edgecomb

Kathryn Edgecombe spends as much time as possible in her writing cabin by the pond. Her work has appeared in several journals and anthologies, and she has published three books of poetry, Not the First Waltz, Midwives to Our Selves, *and* Draw Me to the Flame.

So Happy To Be

"...so happy to be where they are..." – Mary Oliver

At first to be forced behind closed doors
Face masked like a fugitive
   hands covering finger prints
   seemed like a moment of imprisonment

Then –

Time to catch up to one's
   life without interruption –
   to read, clean out clutter
To sweep out the hoardings
   of a too complicated existence
An interval in which to imagine
   words collecting on a page
   a rhapsody of delight
A gift of quietude
   second coffee steaming
   pen poised over page
It hovers in space waiting
   for something more than
   inspiration

Maybe another walk on deserted
   country roads

Kelpie

Tom Vaine

Tom Vaine lives in Elora, Ontario, and works as a high school teacher. He has a graduate degree in Literature Studies, with a focus on speculative fiction. Tom's work has appeared in Bewildering Stories *magazine as well as* Rhapsody, *Guelph's annual poetry collection.*

Kelpie

It turned your knuckles white to see it,
mad eyes rolling, rising from the muck
to stand before you at the water's edge,
its muzzle dripping filth,
and yet its coat was shining dark,
velvet dark,
dark as drowning, beautifully dark and silent
as the depths of the lake, and you knew
when you touched it where it meant to take you,
knew by the song it sang that it would drag you down
as you rode it, pull you under, flooding even your pores
as it devoured you, that despite your desperation
you wouldn't even scream.
That letting others see it would only make it worse.

The Symphonic River

Jerry Prager

Jerry Prager is the author of three volumes on the Calabrian mafia of Guelph, Legends of the Morgeti; *three volumes on on fugitive slaves and how they came to Wellington County; several books of poetry; and is working on a novel series.*

The Symphonic River

The symphonic river plays both sides of the bridge,
the flow of the gathering descent softly erupts
in white cap resistance to submerged rock, a gentle,
reiterated resonance heard under the concrete road span,
the lyric arches on each side posted with listening chambers.

The fall over limestone ledge levels
are accented with cascades of plummeting scales
across last year's rushes and grasses, effervescent cadences,
improvised gurgles and plops, whooshes,
plunges and sprays that whisper downstream and escape hearing:
variations of nuance layering the soundscapes,
isolating strains of melody from the air.

Too diverse for fixation, too alive for inattention,
the symphonic river plays both sides of the bridge
conducted by water levels over the bed of its movements,
themes of melt-flood voice solitudes of winter, internalizing
the virtuosity of a bend crossed by a country road.

And now, hours later, days later, an exuberant tranquility
continues to heal my inner ear – aching from the work
of mallet on chisel on stone – through nothing more than
memories of the hot sun of that sparkling afternoon alone on
a rural shoulder near Irvine Street farm fields, remain
as moments recalled: the cool shadows of the cedar-lined banks
and the receding flood plains;
instants of the awakening Earth relived, like the chorus of insects

thrumming counterpoint to the rolling valley runoff
wash over me like a balm still, long after leaving
the lyric bridge and the symphonic river
and the glorious light of fleeting impressions,
harnessed now to the page for the sake of spoken song
and the traces that you bring to the verses
of your own winter resolves.

every town needs a poet

Morvern McNie

*Morvern McNie writes poetry and short fiction. She has performed at events like the Hillside Festival and the Eden Mills Fringe. Her work has appeared on two Guelph compilation CD's,*Work Songs *and* 60 Second Songs. *She has published chapbook of poetry,* Fish What Youe Lure *(Vocamus Press 2020.)*

every town needs a poet

the old hall is hopping
festooned with loops of paper crepe
bargain balloons to blow and break.
the Fiddler and his befuddled
taking tickets at the door
roasted rump with gravy and mash.
cups of this and cups of that
crank and croon of Fish What You Lure
an ironic mix of salty and sweet
songs from the coast to tempt
the water ghosts from your inland ears

everyone you ever want to see
and everyone you don't want to see
and those in between

there's Harold
tumbling his thoughts
by the washroom door
his hints of conversation
precious stones in a tangled net

Ella and Eleanor in their pleasing polka dots
running their fingers along Jake's tattooed wings
trying to feather his interest with all they know
who's been caught in the long river grass
what is dirty but not obscene
and how some people think that Wilde's Salome
and her dance of the seven veils
is the origin of the striptease

but it's Genevieve
in her red-rimmed specs
dipping her hand into her back pocket
to take out her mini moleskin
to add a few words

she took a bus
from the city of saints
to visit Aunt Heloise
who plays her squeezebox
under her wistful willow tree

Genevieve
Jake wants to know

Hope

Melinda Burns

Melinda Burns is a writer and a psychotherapist in private practice in Guelph, Ontario, where she also teaches writing. She has published poems in various magazines, read her essays on CBC radio, and published essays on writing in Canadian Notes and Queries and in K.D. Miller's Holy Writ. Melinda lives in Guelph, Ontario.

Hope

Hope is such a feathery thing,
fragile and easily felled
for a time

Four years ago, the great despair
that such a person could be
put in charge, that hope was
an illusion, foolish in the face
of terrible reality

So must people have felt
in wartime, how could
the world have come to this?

And then a sea-change
in a country not ours,
and then a riot, and then
a surge ahead, executive
orders slashing across the old regime

righting the ship of state,
the state of the world still
tempest-tossed, and yet

a young Black woman
moved the nation, with
her poem of hope as
mighty
as a sword, a miracle
of words to bind

standing in her yellow coat
like a flame on the
once-stormed steps

Dining in Restaurant

Sheri Doyle

Sheri Doyle is an editor and author who works with educational publishers, trade publishers, and individual authors. She also writes poetry and fiction. She has published a chapbook of poetry, A Dress Made from Light *(Vocamus Press, 2022).*

Dining in Restaurant

In the company of strangers,
who spoke softly by the window
across tables for two at dusk
I lost her a year ago today, cheers to her
or laughed uncontrollably over at the bar
only you would get this, man
or where whispers swept our necks and earlobes,
was the close exchange of words
of air and breath from moving lips.
All of us packed into the restaurant,
shoulder to shoulder, back to back
sometimes just inches apart,
we were faces above candlelight,
eyes in a flare, strange but connected
glances so close that we could see
the flecks of gold in deep brown,
the glint of blue in grey.

We could have eaten at home
but we ate together in crowded rooms
not to hold or know each other
but to exist near one another
as if to close the distances between us,
to feel the light in our shared darkness –
the way we might together hold the moon
lifting now above buildings on these quiet streets.

Oncolomancy

Jeremy Luke Hill

Jeremy Luke Hill is the publisher at Gordon Hill Press and the Managing Director at Vocamus Writers Community. He is the author of several chapbooks of poetry, most recently, Ordinary Eternal Machinery *(845 Press, 2021).*

Oncolomancy

They read the future in her blood,
the thin red lines – how slowly veins
empty if they are opened just
so. Perhaps a slight incision
behind the ear, where heartbeats will
echo when they hang her head down
and let the drops cast a spattered
prognostication in the dust.

Perhaps better to auger the gut,
entreat its entrails to tell her days,
let intestinal knowledge
uncoil between their fingers,
trace the veining fates that river
and embranch her organs to enumerate
the years her heart may have known.

May 4, 2020 Poem

Sandy Bassie

Sandy Bassie has maintained a love of language and a passion for writing her entire life. She reveals this in her journals, reflections on life, poetry, and some (very) short stories

May 4, 2020 Poem

I did not know tears came to poetry, words on a page
someone wrote tell my life back to me. Disrobing

their own for my perusal. Don't be afraid.

Life like tears unplanned to the watering of day
to rising, a pool from low lying ground engorged

emotion / tears blackened / years of peat
colouring their exit and entry

Tears unevened, a machine rusting, sounds irritate

everything my dad taught me about washing
my face was right. My mom teaching me to break

zits and pop blackheads, how not to back away
while she forced my skin to let go

satisfaction rising to each new burst

still my tears exchange outer dams for inner
as the levers are laid out fear / grief / uncertainty / remorse.

My gut, eyes, elbows, knees seize
where instinct used to lie, waiting to run

at the first signs of danger
you taught it to lie, telling me that love is obligation

obedience stays / quiet / conscience holding its breath

To the Resident of the House at the Top of Dublin St.

Kate MacDonald

Kate MacDonald is a graduate from the University of Guelph, where she obtained her BA in English and Creative Writing, and where she currently lives. Her work can be found in the Guelph undergraduate magazine, Kaleidoscope, *and the Alberta based,* WordCity Monthly.

To the Resident of the House at the Top of Dublin St.

Tucked in the back of my drawers,
I've kept them.
Presents, like snapshots left to fade in their frames,
tissue paper gone stale.
I've bottled the feeling of floating down city streets
in the back of your white Chevy,
your cigarette smoke in my hair,
I intended for us to get drunk off it together.
Wrapped in blue ribbons are the echoes
of your Nona's old records saying,
Darling, so it goes.
I've nurtured violets in my flower beds, pressed them; dye for
    your hair.
Every soon has been spun into wool, braided into a blanket
    for sleepless nights.
I'll keep them,
waiting for the next time
our palms embrace.

Getting Through

Donna McCaw

Donna McCaw has written six books, most recently, Across the Great Divide. *She organized Wordfest in April and October at the Elora Centre for the Arts, and does storytelling at various venues.*

Getting Through

Some do leather and pointy studs
Others stilettos and tattoos
Some do organic everything with marijuana buds
Others do Kentucky Fried with booze
Some do eating disorders and anxiety

Others do hair shirts or obesity
What do you do
To get yourself through?

Some do too cool to play the fool
Others do the First Card of the Tarot
Some do the mansion with the pool
Others keep their lives and thinking narrow
Some take that jagged little pill
That inner hole to fill

What do you do
To get yourself through?

Yoga? Green Tea?
Heroin? Harlequins?
Meditation? Codependency?
Cutting? Multiple sins?
Or is it Poetry?
Or do you just let it be?

Back Then

Michael Kleiza

Originally from Montreal, Michael Kleiza now lives in Guelph. Michael's poems have been published in various anthologies and magazines. His first collection of poetry, A Poet on the Moon *(Vocamsu Press), was published in 2015.*

Back Then

Back then he was the lifefull meadows, fields of stone, the
    goldenrod and granite, the burdock and the overburden,
    the jar that glugged the fertile muck of the pond to
    catch water bugs.
Back then he was night sky stars, Orion's belt, the Big
    Dipper, Polaris, galaxies receding, the evening heat,
    lightening lashing the horizon.
Back then he was the wind, the May air, the sun, the
    river and the bent reeds. the shoreline curved, the
    aerodynamics of dragonflies, burping frogs and birds
    spearing the air, the rust on fishhooks in the weeds, all
    the cycles that fall in upon themselves and return.
Back then there were the older boys that had found a robin's
    nest, dropped the chicks one by one into the water
    pushing them under and he hid with death beneath the
    prehistoric tree canopies near the burned-out cars and
    the garbage.
Back then there was the aftermath of a torture that grasped
    tongues, keeping him silent from saying what he saw,
    submerging all that had been done in backrooms where
    the black robes hung.

Silent Killer

Darcy Hiltz

Darcy Hiltz is an Archivist / Librarian at Guelph Public Library. He writes, through his FaceBook profile, about genealogy and information management, and in his spare time he writes poetry. He is married and lives in Fergus, Ontario.

Silent Killer

cannot be seen
sanitizing
washing hands
twenty second frequency
green tape
lines
keep me away
from the person
in front
behind
email, text
zoom
to find the
pulse of a colleague
breath
life beyond 111111's
000000's
bubble-like island
where dreams and thoughts
begin anew

Memorial for a Nameless Matriarch

Shayne Coffin

Shayne Coffin was born and raised in Guelph, Ontario. He attended Fanshawe College in London, graduating from their Theatre Arts program. His poetry has appeared in Fresh Voices *and the 2020 chapbook anthology* Tending the Fire, *both released through the League of Canadian Poets. He has self published six poetry collections, his most recent being* Cabinet Cards *(2022, Volumes Publishing). He currently resides in Harriston.*

Memorial for a Nameless Matriarch

(To a pioneer of old Puslinch, re-interred in Farnham Cemetery, Arkell)

Denied the perfect health of youth,
Run ragged with the biblical expectations of her sex,
Middle-aged daughter, founding mother returned to the dirt she
  toiled,
Declined the eternal leisure of sweet hereafter,
Raised out of sleep beneath her homestead burial,
Weather-stained bones tumble in the hauler, clang inside her
  abductor,
Dumping her miniscule traces with a myriad of other residues
  in the fill,
For how long out of the shelter does she endure the desecration?
Too long, displaced from the result of her labours,
Unearthed, replanted among a prosperous name,
Overshadowed by their illustrious displays of wealth and legacy,
She remains unknown, flat in the grass, looking up to a
  monarch in the trees.

Mouth

Valerie Senyk

Valerie Senyk is a writer, multi-media artist, a playwright, an actor, and a performance poet. She has published a full-length volume of poetry, I Want A Poem *(Vocamus Press, 2014).*

Mouth

Your mouth is full of the unspoken
like an ice jamb behind your teeth,
words jostle each other for room
and keep your tongue swollen

what to say, and then when,
when fewness of words is laudable;
these crawl back into your throat
like chastened children

deep into your belly they swarm
where thousands of infant letters
rebel against their unbirth,
mewling and crying 'I am!'

mouth subdued, inner voice rails
at the clenching of teeth and lips,
rigidity of tongue, a waste
this carousel of words that fail

This was your way times past
your learning was deep and
and it kept you dark and safe;
now let words pass your lips at last

Lost Poetry

Trish Heyes

Trish Heyes is a writer of fiction, poetry and personal essays. Previously her poems have been published in Quills *and* Ascent Aspirations *magazines. Her essays have been published online with* ThoughtCatalog *by One Thousand Trees.*

Lost Poetry

You've lost the poetry.
Either you haven't looked for it yet
or you have decided not to care.
Either way, Regret is on the road to your house.
Before she arrives you will feel the reverb of hooves
a trembling earth
coming for your witnessing.
You will search for it then:
pat down your pockets
flip through your wallet
dig in the crevices between the cushions of your sofa
and the drawer beside your bed.
Casting aside the curtain
there will be no verdant green landscape
to coax your pulse

It is a vast barren now
no magic or miracles
no delight
from stories that are woven so well
that they wind themselves around you
like a cincture,
torturing you like a saint.
But for your gilded house of straw,
you are withered
drought ravaged in your thirst.

How to Survive Winter (Tip #12)

Serena Tene

Serena Tene is a writer of poetry. She has also published many articles on various topics, especially related to environmental, food system, and social justice issues, and she has worked for decades as a communications professional in the non-profit sector.

How to Survive Winter (Tip #12)

Search for a laundromat with southern exposure.
Wait for a sunny day.

(Because your tiny apartment gets only the last bits
of the western sun and you are sun starved.)

Arrive at the laundromat by 10 am
and throw your laundry into the washer.
Collapse joyously in front of the SPECIAL WINDOW
in just. the. right. spot.

Let the full heat and light of the sun
bathe your body and melt your brain.
Notice that you have stopped thinking.

(Because there is no point right now in thinking
about how you are going to pay rent in a few months.)

Learn to love – or ignore – the classic hits
that waft through the laundromat's radio.
Be pleasantly surprised that you now believe
Culture Club was pretty good.

Watch the hot man carrying a white basket
descend from his white truck.
Giggle as a bus covered in an advertisement
for the Love Shop passes by.

Fold your laundry and try not to notice
that your clothes have seen much better days.
Throw away one turquoise t-shirt
you cannot justify wearing any longer.

Leave the laundromat with a slight sunburn
and a great sense of accomplishment.
Hurry home to write this poem
because sun makes you want to write poetry.

For Pam

Catherine Reilly

Catherine Reilly hails originally from Toronto and currently lives in Guelph. Her background in fine art, health science, theological studies and music often appear as themes in her poetry and fiction. She holds a certificate in Creative Writing from the University of Guelph.

For Pam

Walking a dirt path
the day I learned you were gone
my stomach knotted, tangled,
and churned to absorb

the news made me search for you
up in the sky. I knew you were there in the sunlight
caressing my hair as I stood and stared,
at the crimson fall leaves that danced in the air

That night a full moon lit up the inky sky
highlighting your route through the clouds as you flew by
atop the wings of seraphim dressed in rubies and pearls
guiding you to your final resting place high above this world.

Your head was adorned with shimmering gold curls
the heavens a backdrop to the scene unfurled
Oh joy, a new star has arrived, sang the celestial
chorus. She is finally at peace here amongst us

Back on earth , upon terra firma
my feet encased in blue and brown wool
the socks you created
the warmth in my toes equals that in my heart,
forever grateful for your friendship
this aggrieved morsel I impart.

Am I

Darcy Hiltz

Darcy Hiltz is an Archivist / Librarian at Guelph Public Library. He writes, through his FaceBook profile, about genealogy and information management, and in his spare time he writes poetry. He is married and lives in Fergus, Ontario.

Am I

empathic
intelligent
conscientious

em p th c + 2 vowels
int ll g nt + 3 vowels
c + 5 vowels and 7

merely consonants
that mix with

a
e i
o u

sometimes
            y

sounds
obstruct
breath

I am

Immanence

Marian Thorpe

Marian Thorpe is a writer of historical and urban fantasy. Her works include the Empire's Legacy *series, historical fantasy set in an analogue of northern Europe after the decline of the Roman Empire, and* In An Absent Dream, *an urban fantasy chapbook (Vocamus Press 2018).*

Immanence

I don't know where I was. Arkansas, maybe? A National Wildlife Refuge, a weekday morning in July, no one else around. A flat land, bisected by water. Wide trails, wide enough for a vehicle, thick vegetation on either side.

The air was heavy with moisture and the smell of DEET. Long sleeves, long trousers tucked into socks against ticks. I was walking slowly, birding, and anyhow, it was too humid to do anything else.

What made me turn? Probably I'd stopped to look at a bird. Probably my glasses had steamed up, and I'd lowered my binoculars and moved my head to make a little breeze. I looked behind me, the way I'd come.

The cat emerged from the vegetation, saw me, stopped. My breath caught. We stared at each other. Its golden eyes blinked, muscles tensed for movement. I was the interloper, the one being assessed. The cat belonged here. We watched each other for heartbeats, breaths.

Without hurry, the cat glided across the path and into the grasses. Gone, leaving only its shape in my memory; shape and movement, golden eyes, spotted fur.

And something theoretical had become real, an idea made tangible, a word made flesh. *Bobcat.*

Saturday Special

Anne Walk

After studying visual art at the University of Western Ontario, Anne Walk went on hiatus before embarking on a career in writing. Anne is of mixed heritage, Haudenosaunee (Cayuga) and Hungarian, and is currently living in Guelph, Ontario. She has been published in Room Magazine *and is the second place winner of the Humber Literary Review's 2022 Emerging Fiction Writers contest.*

Saturday Special

"Beauty!" says the wheat blond man with his checkered shirt tucked into the back of his sagging jeans. He's inspecting a statue, carved oak, fringed and feathered, one hand raised like a visor, skin stained red.

Another man, white haired, looks up from a chair under a blue tarp next to a jacked up four by four.

It's the last Antique Market of the season and the white-haired man needs a sale. He advances slowly, sussing out the customer with a wary eye.

"Where'd you get it?" asks the blond man.

"Oh, at some auction or other."

The white-haired man stands beside the statue and slaps a hand down on its wooden shoulder.

"You don't see a lot of these anymore," says Blondie. He shakes his head.

"No, well, you know. Like I said. It was an auction." Whitey juts his chin out, stands tall, buries his fists in his front pockets.

They eye each other for a moment, the statue between them.

"My granddad used to have something similar when I was a kid." says Blondie with a nervous chuckle.

"Issat so?" Whitey's posture relaxes. He looks at his watch, looks up at the setting sun.

"Yeah. Part of a wild west theme he had going on in his den. He was a real collector. I grew up just over there

31

off Gilmour." Blondie looks in the direction of the road and Whitey turns and looks with him.

Standing side by side, they could be brothers.

"How much are you asking?" Blondie looks the statue up and down, his gaze lingering here and there, settling on the stoic mouth. He leans into the face, notes the curve of the nose, raises a finger and traces the war paint on its cheeks.

"I'm asking a thousand."

"A thousand? That seems steep for what it is." Blondie rubs the flat top of the cigar bundle in the statue's hand. "It needs a fresh coat of paint." He'll put it at the front door, use it to catch his keys when he comes in.

"I'll give you five hundred."

The other vendors start packing up. Whitey sighs and says, "Eight hundred. Any less and I might as well keep it myself. Take it over to Niagara Falls next month where I can get twelve."

Blondie shifts from foot to foot, kicks at the dirt, considering. Eight hundred is a lot for what it is. But he nods. He'll take it. And Whitey smiles and heads over to the truck to get his iPad.

"Do you have a tarp?" Blondie shouts over. "Don't need any trouble on the ride home. You know how some people are."

"Sure thing," says Whitey. He gives Blondie a sympathetic pat on the back. "No extra charge.

Where are you parked? I'll help you carry it over. It's a bit of a beast."

They both laugh.

"Thanks, man. You're a good guy."

"Thanks," says Whitey. "I try to be."

Vocamus Writers Community

Vocamus Writers Community is a non-profit community organization that supports book culture in Wellington County. It runs workshops, writing groups, and writer hang-outs. It offers resources for writers looking to publish their work both traditionally and independently. It promotes readings, launches, and other literary events in the community. It also produces the annual *Rhapsody* anthology of Guelph area writing. For more information, email vocamuswriterscommunity@gmail.com.

www.ingramcontent.com/pod-product-compliance
Lightning Source LLC
Chambersburg PA
CBHW051713090426
42736CB00013B/2675